EVERYONE IS CREATIVE

What do we need to be creat

Actually we already have the
them with us every day – our eyes.

All that's required is that we see, use our vision and
accurately record the world around us.

Nothing more is needed.

This book offers some suggestions for developing your
ability to see – where to place emphasis, what to look
at, where to start. Always encouraging you to develop
your 'unique eye', a vision of the world that I believe
you already innately possess.

Everyone is creative.

Everyone is creative, whether they admit it or not,
whether they accept it or not.

So try being an 'artist', embrace the 'A' word. Look
around – what is happening right now in front of you?

Try it.

What have you got to lose?

EVERY-
ONE
IS
CREATIVE

MICHAEL ATAVAR

Kiosk Publishing

info@everyone-is-creative.com
www.everyone-is-creative.com

ISBN 978-0-9531073-3-9
A catalogue record for this book is available
from the British Library.

Artwork by Richard Scarborough
Typeset in Trade Gothic

Facio mundum

How do you start? Just open your eyes.

CONTENTS

ONE IDEA

One Idea	2
On Your Own	4
Basics	8
Rucksack	12
Leave The Stage Empty	16

MATERIALS

I Start With Materials	22
If You Think...	26
Sensuality & Surface	30
Use You	34
Emergence & Risk	38
Factory Blue	42
Foggy Landscape	46

ARTIST'S STATEMENT

I Believe	52
A Piece Of Fiction	56
10 People	60
Fireworks	64
Write In Reverse	68
Chop Wood	72

MANIFESTO

You Are Not Alone	78
Anti-You	82
This Page Is Left Blank	86
Draw Blood	90

THINK SMALL

Think Small	96
100 - 1%	100
Playing Scales	102
Blurred Pictures	106
Offending The Audience	110

UNIQUE EYE

Unique Eye	116
One Book	120
Nothing To Say (I Don't Believe You)	124
X-Rays	128
Poor Art	132
Write It Down	136
I'm Drawn To Ideas X, Y, Z	140

SEEING

Seeing	146
Taboo Against Looking	150
What Do I See?	154
Use Whatever Is Already There	158

IMAGES

An Opening Into You	162
Draw Approximations	166
The Desert	170
Wild Horses On The Wall	174
Found Material	178
Le 'C' Dream	182
The Reverse	186

I SEE

A Glass On A Table	192
Rods	196
I See A Palm Tree	200
Long Stories	204
Laser Cone	208
Ishihara	212

EVERYONE IS CREATIVE

Art Is...	216
Rhododendrons	218
Dirty Water	222
The Fountain	226
Close Your Eyes	230

ACKNOWLEDGEMENTS

	233

ONE IDEA

ONE IDEA

We are all working with one idea, turning this way and that to get a new angle, another take on our basic material.

Sometimes we can spend our whole lives exploring this one theme.

However, it's not easy. It requires –

- Persistence.
- Feats of bravery.
- Conceptual acuity.
- Iconoclasm.

But don't worry if you don't have these qualities. If you keep going, you will learn them over time. The act of being creative will teach you everything that you need to know about –

- People.
- Situations.
- Relationships.
- Dynamics.

If you explore your one idea in all its detail and depth, everything will come to you.

Stay with it...

And see.

We are all working with one idea.

ON YOUR OWN

You are here, quite on your own.

But don't worry. That's OK. It's always where you begin as an artist, with your own resources.

If you can learn to use these basics, you will have a toolkit that you can always draw on in the future to make work.

In fact, the process is always about going back to these first principles each time for inspiration and advice.

You don't need fancy apparatus, or the latest thing, to create your artwork. The simplest items will do.

- Paper.
- Eye.
- Pen.
- Hand.

It's possible to scale these up later on, when you output, in order to make a more commercial product. But your work can also be exhibited without these things.

I remember once when I was in Berlin, I saw a series of A5 felt-tip pen drawings, all displayed on the wall of a domestic interior. There were probably thirty of them, each a remembered scene, a snapshot from the artist's walk in the city.

Because the material was intrinsically interesting,
the output needed to be nothing more than the pages
from his notepad pinned to the wall.

Seeing this exhibition reminded me that everyone can
connect with the everyday details of a life, accurately
described.

For example, when I wrote about my own existence
with all the details of my urban life left intact, people
were attracted to this frankness of style; it hadn't been
said before so people listened.

The more that you can draw on the specifics, with all
the good and the bad things left unexpurgated, the
more universal your work will appear.

The more you can be yourself, the more successful
you will become.

Paradoxically this always works.

You are alone – but don't worry. You carry everything
with you inside.

The more you can be yourself, the more successful you will become.

BASICS

I like the basics range currently available in my local supermarket, the no frills version of tissues, bread, light bulbs and baked beans.

I always enjoy seeing these packets because they remind me of the basics of art practice, the building blocks.

Nothing too fancy, just the beginnings of an idea.

- Yourself.
- A microphone.
- Other people.
- A space.

Even some of these are not necessary; other people are a luxury.

You can make work now on your own. Just use your body in space as the resource.

- Heart.
- Eyes.
- Height.
- Breath.
- Ears.

Try your voice out.

It can go from a whisper to a loud shout.

Express yourself with this vocal range. Add a microphone and double its volume. Quadruple it in size.

Let your voice fill the whole room.

Released from the expectations of what creativity ought to be, forced to build a new relationship with materials, what would you choose to do?

Creativity is nothing other than your personality writ large.

Released from the expectations of what creativity ought to be, what would you choose to do?

RUCKSACK

If I were stranded on a desert island, these are the things I would need in my rucksack to encourage my creativity.

Artist's Basic Toolkit

- Pen.
- Notepad.
- Battery operated Dictaphone (for recording interviews or listening to your own voice).
- Microphone.
- Dice (for making random choices).
- Scissors and glue (for cut-ups).
- Paint.
- Table (for working at).
- Digital pocket camera (as a notepad).

Update using any contemporary technology.

None of this needs to be 'the best'. It's good to use excellent materials, but don't allow a lack of money to stop you from starting.

Just begin with what you have.

For example, a cheap camera is best, rather than a large deluxe version. Also, pocket-sized is good, so that you start to carry these items around with you all the time.

You need to get into a practice of working wherever you are, with the materials that are to hand.

Try some of the following processes to adapt any idea that you have, transforming it into new material.

- Turn it upside down.
- Superimpose ideas.
- Add inexplicable events.
- Reverse the time chronology.
- Splice together opposite elements.
- Change the authorial voice.
- Slow down/speed up.
- Use parallel events.

Once you have an idea, your concept is transferable to any format, outside your notepad, through any means necessary.

The limit is merely the frontier of your imagination.

Don't allow a lack of money to stop you from starting. Just begin with what you have.

LEAVE THE STAGE EMPTY

I once ran a course that culminated in a series of performances. However, the college where I was working had few resources to offer the students. Instead, during the end of term showcase, the classmates used the desks like barricades and turned the strip lighting on and off, dramatically illuminating the scene.

It was very inspiring.

It reminds me that anything can be made with the materials that you see around you.

- Four chairs.
- A light bulb.
- A pair of scissors.
- A newspaper.
- Brooms.

In fact, you can only begin here.

Top Tip
Leave the stage empty.

Don't fill it up with domestic scenery. Leave it vast, metaphorical.

If you need to create walls, do it with light instead. The stark scenery that comes with darkness or brilliant white light is beyond compare.

Use resources like scraps, suggesting something rather than stating it upfront.

Give the viewer space to occupy the work themselves.

Cut holes for them to breathe.

Give the viewer space to occupy the work themselves.

MATERIALS

I START WITH MATERIALS

I often start with materials.

These are the kinds of household basics that you find anywhere –

- A black felt-tip.
- White lined index cards.
- An 80 leaf ring-bound notepad.
- A yellow highlighter pen.
- A5 size plastic bags.
- Rubber bands.

I use the felt-tip to write in the notepad, whilst I make notes on the index cards, with some lines underlined with the yellow highlighter. The bags keep the cards clean.

At the next level of my practice I use –

- *I Ching.*
- Dice.
- A hat.
- Coloured hexagrams (bought at a flea market).
- A book.

The *I Ching* (an ancient Chinese form of divination) is used to find out what's happening in my interior life, whilst the dice, hat and book all support me in making random selections from a series of choices.

Lastly, the hexagrams, shaken in a bag, help me to choose colours.

These are all the materials I need.

I have a computer, but if I didn't have access to microchips or electricity, I would work by hand, assembling copies of my books using old technology.

Creativity comes out of sophisticated adaptation, not expensive investment.

Rubber bands hold things together.

Creativity
comes out of
sophisticated
adaptation,
not expensive
investment.

IF YOU THINK...

If you think that these are absurd choices, that there must be more to creativity than this...

Be careful.

No tools need to be any more sophisticated than the ones on my list.

We can sometime use expensive equipment to build barriers, bigger walls of defence against the moment when we have to start – make a mark, a sentence, a line. I try to avoid this by only working with simple materials. Here, at least, there's no place to hide.

I work on paper first.

The fluidity of the blank page always surprises me.

If I want to extend my ideas, I just tape more sheets together to make a small book, a poster or a giant newspaper.

The principles are always the same – a series of small moves added together in modular fashion over time, that's all creativity is.

For example, I recently bought a cheap knitted wool blanket in a charity shop. It comprises 8 x 9 squares. A total of 72 units, made up of 22 random colours.

It reminds me of the drawing experiments of Sol LeWitt, where he applied the pencil directly to the gallery wall.

Therefore, my 70s blanket inspires me, taking me back to the basics of practice – complementary shapes, juggled together in myriad forms.

It tells me that all creativity, however complex, can be mapped through a series of small squares, individually stitched.

The Exercise

Make a book of twelve pages.

Create a volume of scraps, with no element bigger than one side of paper.

The book can be A5, A4, A3 all the way up to A0 (119 x 84 cm).

Make it bigger; make it the size of this room.

Only work with simple materials. Here, at least, there's no place to hide.

SENSUALITY & SURFACE

Materials help us cut through our creative blocks.

If we pay attention to their sensuality and surface, we do not need to generate ideas. The materials will create them for us.

They will help us push through.

Our close-up observation of their qualities –

- Toughness
- Pliability
- Irregularity
- Playfulness
- Solidity

will open up feelings of hope, clarity and fear in us.

These we can adapt, modify or amplify to develop creative ideas.

For example, even within the limits of white paper, there is a variety of possibilities – tones and weight, texture and size.

I could create a practice based on simple sheets of blank paper.

(I'm excited.)

Or –

- Plastic.
- Gloss paint.
- Fabric.
- Tile.
- Cardboard.
- Video.

None of these needs to be expensive.

Often, useful items can be found abandoned on the street. Even in the city, you can find discarded wooden chairs, half-empty paint cans and old kitchen cabinets.

Try some of these.

In the past, I was quite willing to fool myself into believing that unless certain conditions were present, then I couldn't start.

The reality was that I didn't want to begin.

Instead, I'm now building a new relationship with materials – a blanket, cardboard packing boxes, paper, a child's adventure book, a blue bag.

These I explore in complex ways – putting the parts together in multiple combinations.

Top Tip

In order to get in touch with the quality of things, try touching them.

Touch is very underrated.

It can move you rapidly towards a feeling that you haven't experienced before, a sensation in the body that's hard to ignore.

The sensate surface of things offers us a lot of undiscovered potential that we can use in our work.

Put your fingers on something.

How does it feel?

Materials help us cut through our creative blocks.

USE YOU

If you want something to happen, try doing it yourself first.

Put you in there.

Sometimes we want to be creative but we imagine that without really trying, by some stroke of magic, we will become inspired, without having to apply ourselves.

This never happens.

Instead, make the experiment with yourself, as the first stage of your creativity.

For example, if you want to write about a runner, learn to run. If your play is about isolation, draw the curtains for a week. If you want to paint abstracts, remove the figurative from your environment.

This is not to deny the strength of the imagination to power us towards our dreams, however, these basic steps, engaging 'I', will allow you to embody your ideas in yourself, as a first testing ground.

And keep the experiment real.

I once worked with a client whose imagery was based on bridges. I encouraged her to visit as many types of bridge as she could and to write about the experience when she was there.

Make the bridge a 'bridge' into something new.

These active engagements with the physical, grounding you in the world, are an intrinsic part of being creative.

Otherwise we can sometimes become drifting, remote.

- Hold materials.
- Put your feet on the floor.
- Find a base.

Here at least is solid ground.

Make the experiment with yourself, as the first stage of your creativity.

EMERGENCE & RISK

Sometimes I find that one small item can trigger a whole ricochet of ideas.

These objects are often found for free, on the street, or if paid for, cost little more than a few pence.

So I stay alert to subtle changes in the environment, paying particular attention to materials that jar with the landscape.

For example, as a test, I might follow a white plastic bag on its journey down the street, buoyed up by the currents, drifting in space. Or, alternatively, I could set in motion a similar experiment and record the event, with me as a part of the action, photographing the results.

Art is about intention; the willingness to be seen.

Such experiments, like the one above, place you, the maker, in a position of tension, where you become visible to everyone around you.

Even in the city, people will point and stare.

But this embarrassment that you feel is good. It indicates that you are ready to be seen as a creative person, regardless of what others think.

Therefore, every time you have a good idea, stop in the street and write it in your notepad. Note it down before it escapes.

Don't worry if everyone looks at you.

You are creative; it's part of your job.

Top Tip
The physical is the only portal we have into the unknown.

Copy the magicians of old and repeat things until you are dizzy with transcendence.

The chord of C, played in an arpeggio over and over again, very rapidly for ten minutes, will take you anywhere you need to go.

Remember, art sometimes equals physical endurance.

(Take suitable precautions.)

Art sometimes equals physical endurance.

FACTORY BLUE

Materials, by their very qualities, often offer us a way forward.

- Colour.
- Surface.
- Limitations.
- Size.

Why fight it?

If you need to use blue, use the most basic blue that you can find – a blue that might emerge from a factory.

I remember once I heard a story about the artist Félix Gonzáles-Torres. When he made one of his paper stack sculptures, he asked the factory to deliver the paper in the colour 'blue'.

Whatever arrived, he accepted.

I've had this happen to me several times in my career.

When the first edition of 'How To Be An Artist' came back from the printers, it was the wrong size – the factory had simply realigned the text to suit a larger format.

It looked better than the size I had intended, so I just paid for it without any questions asked.

Top Tip
Use default settings and innate elements to offer
yourself ready-made solutions to complex problems.

Don't struggle.

So if like Marcel Duchamp's 'The Large Glass' your
sculpture comes back from transit with large cracks all
over, exhibit it anyway, as seen, without any attempt to
fix it, using the random properties added on its journey,
to enhance the piece by adding further complexity.

Drop your decisions and let the materials speak for
themselves.

What might they say?

Don't struggle.

FOGGY LANDSCAPE

As I write this, I am on a train heading south, travelling through a foggy landscape.

I look out into the white banks of mist.

It reminds me that in creativity, the purpose is often obscure: we don't know what we're doing. Creative thinking is just like that. It's full of mysterious reasoning.

Often it's helpful just to accept that you are lost.

I usually don't find out what's happening to me until much later, once the process is over. Sometimes it takes me years to understand my motivation for making something.

The other thing that occurs to me is the need to internalise outside experiences, to use these events and fold them back into my practice.

The fog tells me something quite interesting about myself – obscurity rising, fog banks, things becoming hidden.

If I remain curious about where I am, I can use these physical manifestations to create ideas that help stimulate my work, offering a further layer of meaning.

For example, once I was working with a group, when I suddenly noticed a speck of dust in the centre of the circle, on the carpet. Seeing it, I remarked that even this piece of dirt could help us transform our creativity, if we paid attention to it and pulled it into our world.

It just so happened that in the break, unknown to me, one of the group members had placed the dust there, as a kind of provocation.

He finally joyfully admitted this, acknowledging my discovery of his private art joke.

If you keep your eyes and ears open, anything can give you this inspiration, offering new territory within yourself for exploration.

Even a piece of dirt.

Often it's helpful just to accept that you are lost.

ARTIST'S STATEMENT

I BELIEVE

If you want to write an artist's statement, try using one of these phrases –

Twenty Opening Lines

- I am...
- I dream...
- I'm good at...
- My skill is...
- I believe...
- I'm anti...
- I'm scared of...
- I'm curious about...
- This interests me because...
- The themes of my work are...
- My expertise is...
- The value of my work is...
- My work looks like...
- My work sounds like...
- My work behaves like...
- Historically...
- The context is...
- The landscape is...
- My peers are...
- The critical context is...

'I believe' is a very powerful tool.

Forced to state what your belief system is, you might be surprised at what emerges – optimism, generosity, altruism.

Recently, when I ran this exercise with two sides of a starkly divided company, the shared goals of the organisation came through very strongly, offering some core beliefs that were hard to ignore.

It wasn't exactly healing (some things take more time), however, it revealed the power of 'I believe' to unite the group.

Top Tip
When writing the answers to the above 'twenty opening lines' list, try lying on the floor, making a connection between the power of 'I believe' and the energetic optimism of the child.

Down on the floor, boundaries become more blurred, avoiding the rigidity of upright hierarchical thinking.

Use 'I believe' to transport you back to a time of unrestricted invention, when everything was interesting and alive.

Forced to state

what your belief
system is, you
might be
surprised at
what emerges.

A PIECE OF FICTION

My own artist's statements have varied wildly over time (some of them are still available online if you search hard enough).

They present a somewhat fragmented picture of my personality.

Yet each was 'true' at a particular time.

It reminds me that the artist's statement is a piece of fiction. Not that it's necessarily an outright lie, rather that it represents an imaginative fusion of desire and fact.

These statements are merely the first crude attempts at psychological adaptation, the chance to test the idea out on paper before it occurs in real life.

The Exercise

First, create the context and then make the work that fits the description.

The artist's statement is therefore your intended image written down, at one moment in time, fluid and changeable, full of fantasy and potential.

Use as much imagination to write your statement as you would in the making of your creative work.

Top Tip

In your statement, add a big slogan.

If necessary, create a movement around you to bolster your own voice.

(Especially if it's only you involved.)

Use the plural – 'collective', 'artists', 'institute' – to suggest a veritable art army behind you, supporting you as you go.

The artist's statement is a piece of fiction.

10 PEOPLE

If you can't write your own artist's statement, ask ten people to give you their views on your practice.

This process might reveal something new, something that you were not able to articulate yourself.

Use some of their observations in your final text.

Perhaps they –

- Find a detail.
- Make a statement about scale.
- Note conflicts.
- Reveal your unconscious.
- See humour in unexpected places.
- Offer a sub-text.
- Give you an image.

Let these snapshots form a mosaic, a bigger picture of your work, one that you can't ordinarily see.

Or try another way of working – add a piece about you from a respected critic. Use this journalistic text to indicate the wider context of your practice, placing you in relation to other artists.

Show this article alongside your own artist's statement.

Many times, I'd prefer someone else to write about me, or tell me what I'm doing – offering a perspective that I don't normally have. Most days I'm working close-up, in micro mode, simply fixing something or trying to complete a project. I have no overview whatsoever.

Someone else can give me a bigger context for my work.

Like Andy Warhol, I would give anything for a boss to set my agenda each week.

Top Tip
The '10 people' technique can also be applied to almost any area of life.

Within ten opinions you will get a spread of feedback that will enable you to make a good, balanced decision, based on a variety of views.

Select widely, across the boundaries of class or profession.

If you can't write your own artist's statement, ask ten people to give you their view on your practice.

FIREWORKS

The clever artist doesn't just make a statement using terms that are current, rather they add an extra element, a narrative sophistication, that is truly their own.

Most emerging artists unconsciously don't want to offend anyone. They want to be well received. So they tend to make statements that are too generic. In fact, this does the opposite from what it's intended to do – it makes people switch off.

Instead, what is really interesting are the flaws, the mistakes, the cracks.

These statements, like fireworks going off in front of me, use –

- Brevity
- Injudicious words
- Collision
- Determination
- Odd mismatches
- Visual flair

to grab my attention.

Don't expect that anyone will filter through your CV to find out about you. Package these facts for them in a series of small, highly adapted paragraphs.

Most recipients of artists' statements –

- Don't know you.
- Don't know your work.
- Don't think about your difficulties.
- Don't consider your life.

They simply want to invest in professional proposals and not have their own heads on the line.

Make it easy for them. Remember –

- If your statement is chaotic, you appear out of control.
- If your statement contains no images, you are visually bereft.
- If your statement has no themes, you cannot describe your work.
- If you application is overlong, you have no editing skills.

Why would they give you support if you can't present yourself in a coherent manner?

Top Tip
In a proposal, it's useful to offer some simple things –

- Describe what I might see.
- Offer a list of references.
- Identify the themes of the piece.
- Talk about your motivation.

Don't just describe the content – this feels unsophisticated.

Tell me about the bigger picture. Write about the wider context of your practice, noting in detail the narratives that have emerged over time.

Tell me about you.

(Keep it short.)

Don't just describe the content. Tell me about the bigger picture.

WRITE IN REVERSE

Working forwards is always a difficult task.

It's all about our drive to finish.

We work endlessly to complete a project, with sometimes little thought of what we are actually making. Working forwards often convinces us to use structures that are very predictable – climactic endings and dramatic revelations.

Working forwards is a very masculine idiom, concerned largely with action.

I find these forward-facing structures very unhelpful. They move us step by step, in a mechanical way, towards an inevitable ending.

In life that's not how things happen.

Instead, try writing your piece in reverse. Start from the conclusion and work backwards, in stages, through all the necessary developments that propelled your characters to the final denouement.

This encourages an attitude in you that is less climactic, with a marked absence of drama. You will find yourself concentrating on the background rather than what's upfront.

It's often a more interesting approach.

An even better way to start is from no in-point. Simply explore the environment, in a research-based way, choosing when to narrow the focus and when to take a wide-angle approach.

Use non-hierarchical, backwards-facing models in order to encourage flexibility and unpredictability in your work.

Top Tip
Also try reversing yourself.

If you can start from a place of conclusion, where all the action is over, what might you actually want to say?

If you can start
from a place
of conclusion,
where all the
action is over,
what might you
actually want
to say?

CHOP WOOD

In order to be ourselves, we need to break the self.

Just like the shaman who must snap and reassemble his own bones before he climbs the birch tree up to the stars.

(All a metaphor, of course.)

We have no choice but to systematically remake each part of our spirit, to dissolve the walls of the ego, in order to become new beings...

Or at the very least good artists.

I have done this in the most unlikely places: draughty church halls, early morning starts in the cold snap and dusty backrooms of pubs, sunlight emerging through dirty panes.

This all takes time...

It's a lifetime's work.

And even if I could tell you how to do it, I wouldn't, because that would be counterproductive; you might not hear me.

You would insist on easier solutions.

We all have fantasies about what creativity might be –
how we will respond when we are famous or when we
sell our idea to Hollywood.

However, what creative practice really involves, in a
more pragmatic sense, is a day-to-day commitment
to activity – to sitting at your desk, regardless of
inspiration.

It's only the doingness of doing that makes things
happen –

- Regularity.
- Its step-by-step nature.
- Basic tasks repeated over and over.
- Frequent boredom.
- A long number of words.
- The blank page.

Many times I have sat in front of the computer screen
and not known what to say, but understood that there
were a number of words to be written that day, whether
I wanted to or not.

Out of a lack of words, I still produce words.

So I believe in the long dotted line of days –

- The cold days.
- The good days.
- The intransigent days.
- The slow days.

- The miracle days.
- The broken boiler days.
- The successful days.
- The fast days.

I believe in doing something every day.

I like the original quote from Zen master Wu Li – it's useful to attach it here.

'Before enlightenment, chop wood and carry water. After enlightenment, chop wood and carry water.'

This means that you must physicalise the act, repeat it, regardless of the result. And keep on doing this, as if your life depended on it.

If you can, make your daily practice include –

- Delivering logs
- Cleaning windows
- Washing dishes
- Serving food

then you will give your mind a break, dropping down into the everyday reality of mundane tasks.

Here, you can have some of your best ideas.

It's only
the doingness
of doing that
makes things
happen.

MANIFESTO

YOU ARE NOT ALONE

You are not alone.

Draw some support for yourself from knowledge and context.

It might feel that you are isolated in your struggle, but that's not quite true. Many artists have gone before you, each fighting for their unique relationship with the world.

Just like you they were once attempting to have a visionary experience of art.

If you cannot paint your painting, look at other pictures to find the way forward. Find out about the structural difficulties that other artists have had to overcome.

What would –

- Linda Montano
- On Karawa
- Josef Albers
- Naum Gabo
- Chris Burden
- Nam June Paik

have done?

Become informed.

This discourse, if you can have it, suggests a depth of conscience, an impressive maturity that will win over others to your cause.

You will be able to argue your corner, if you need to.

I often look at 'Silence' by John Cage, 'From A To B And Back Again' by Andy Warhol or 'Grapefruit' by Yoko Ono for inspiration, trying to imagine what these artists might do.

How did they turn things around?

I draw on their strength, their optimism and their humour to support me through the bad times.

Many artists
have gone
before you,
each fighting
for their unique
relationship
with the world.

ANTI-YOU

It's possible to define your creativity by deciding what you are not.

Create a manifesto, detailing all the limits of your practice.

- I will not be X.
- I will not make X.
- I will not exhibit X.
- I will not say X.

Write a manifesto (especially if it's only you).

All art movements are, in fact, usually only one person. They are the outputs of one singular individual.

I've always been inspired by this kind of approach.

My early investigations into art practice were all from a theoretical point of view. Since I was young and didn't know any artists, I spent my time in the local library, soaking up information about Tristan Tzara, Louis Aragon, André Breton and Jean Arp.

I learnt about art from the manifestos of these radicals.

Therefore I've always been drawn to inverse ways of working, negative space, anti-authoritarian processes, the world upside down.

The Exercise

Make a list of twenty things that you don't like in art – perhaps it's portraits, modernism, abstract painting or installation art.

Decide what you don't want to do.

Then look at what's left. Where are the gaps? Is there a sliver of daylight? Your work can often be made in this clear space, in opposition to other approaches.

(With a pair of scissors cut out some space.)

Use this reverse way of working to free you up, to find a form.

But don't worry if there's only 1% left – there is enough here for a lifetime's work. It's these slim pickings, this minor territory, that you can mine to good effect.

Anti-art.
Anti-voice.
Anti-breath.

Begin here, if you can.

Top Tip
In one workshop, a participant asked me to make
something creative out of the book he had brought
with him – Marx and Engels' 'The Communist
Manifesto'.

This was a difficult, though not impossible, task.

The explosive images that he picked at random from
the pages revealed some tension about what tomorrow
might bring. Thus he reminded me that with our
imagination we are always balancing self-awareness
with risk, clarity with questions, knowledge with
uncertainty about the future.

His own manifesto (if he chose to write it) might
include some of these things.

With a pair of
scissors cut out
some space.

THIS PAGE IS LEFT BLANK

Don't try so hard, especially at the beginning of your career.

Your first book/show/play is likely to be everything that you have learned up to that point. You can probably cut it in half, delete 50% and it would still have the same impact.

Try it.

Erase a few of the ideas so that the viewer can find their own feelings.

Sadly, if you fill up all the space, you exclude the possible interpretations of your audience; you deny them the opportunity.

The Exercise

Exclude all the content: back to zero.

Then add in the basic ingredients, one at a time, to find out what's necessary to your story.

Speed up/slow down in your rehearsals to expose these gaps, these grey areas.

Sometimes we use padding to fill up the space, to make ourselves feel safe, like layers of clothing to keep us from the cold.

Must all of it be used?

If you are willing, expose your own relationship to the material, rather than develop stereotypical narratives based on what you don't instinctively know.

Keep it grounded in what you see.

Top Tip
Build your own method of making work and enshrine it in a set of techniques, like Einstürzende Neubauten's instructions pack 'Dave', used for generating ideas, or my own creative deck '210CARDS', a set of tools to inspire new ways of thinking.

Make the system your manifesto.

This page is deliberately left blank.

Sometimes we use padding to fill up the space, to make ourselves feel safe.

DRAW BLOOD

We all have a unique way of seeing, of feeling, of thinking.

We all see the same glass, the same colour, the same water differently; it's a separate shade of blue for everyone.

This original way of seeing is at the centre of our creativity.

In fact our mistakes, our flaws can be the basis of our art, defining our practice by what we are not. I find a deep sense of power in our mistakes, our inabilities – they create our innate sense of style.

So you can't draw? Then make a practice where your attempts, the collapse of the line, your battle with the page become your trademark.

If you also deliver this output with élan, with an act of self-conscious bravery, then your personality, your flair, will attract others.

By the way...

It's not necessary to conform to a blueprint to make money.

Manners, reliability and tact are all useful but they can't replace originality. It's separation from the crowd that will eventually gain you your crown.

If your work doesn't fit the conventions, one way of creating a space for it is to design an alternative world where your products look entirely normal.

- Install a kiosk.
- Open a nightclub.
- Inhabit a temporary shop.
- Build a shack.

Construct a world where your work looks perfectly contextualised –

- A cave.
- A shop with flashing strobe lights.
- An empty garage.
- A balloon ride.

Top Tip

I have lived on the margins of society and found great resources in the values of those on the outside.

I have defined my work by what it's not. (Though this is an all-or-nothing methodology. If you try this approach, please exercise due caution.)

Dress accordingly, in the battledress of the revolutionary, or that of the flâneur, the fop, the freak.

Make work that constantly provokes the mainstream, with a pin stuck in the thumb of society.

Draw blood.

Make work

that constantly
provokes the
mainstream,
with a pin stuck
in the thumb
of society.

THINK SMALL

THINK SMALL

Be afraid of complicating things.

By discounting the simple, you turn away from yourself towards the impossible.

We are complex creatures with complicated levels of denial. We pretend to ourselves that we have honest objections, that we can't do things, that resources are tight, when the truth is that we really fear change and what it might do to our lives.

Don't think big.

Think small.

Processes can help us to do this –

- Upside down.
- Collecting.
- The reverse.
- Timed observations.
- Found objects.
- The automatic.

For example, whilst writing this text, I discover one process here on the page, a found object in the list above – 'Upside down collecting' (the accidental alignment of two separate phrases) – that immediately puts me in new space, one I hadn't thought of before.

What is 'Upside down collecting'?

The idea could become an instruction for me today, to see what I might amass using this method.

How could I collect whilst upside down?

Alternatively, I might turn the word 'collecting' itself upside down and think of the opposite of it – distribution, giving away, abandonment.

So I could offload some old items to provide myself with creative ballast, like throwing sandbags out of a hot air balloon.

What could I get rid of?

Thus by following these hidden clues, I can find some possibilities for new ways of working, ideas I hadn't considered before.

Top Tip
These kinds of word games that I am describing here are the abracadabra, the hey presto of creativity.

They offer magic formulas that can shift our perspective in a single line.

'Hocus pocus', 'Shazam' or even 'Open sesame' – I feel drawn to these magic words, purveyors of destiny, opportunity and change.

Play board games to stimulate your facility with language.

Generate clues but make all the words –

- Colours.
- Rock formations.
- Ice cream flavours.
- Pasta.
- Clouds.
- Metals.
- Capital cities.
- Airlines.

Word games are the abracadabra, the hey presto of creativity.

100 – 1%

Reduce your output by 50%.

What does it look like?

Then take your scissors and cut it in half again and again. Make it 10%. Keep reducing until you reach 1% of the original.

What do you have now?

Is it possible to exhibit these few fragments in a big white space? Can you let go of the 99% and stand naked, unsupported by volume, by padding, reduced to the outline of yourself?

What does 1% look like?

Top Tip
Alternatively, make something out of nothing.

If you require a model, think of Steve Reich's 'Clapping Music', a piece composed of nothing but handclaps.

So you have no musical instruments?

Use your hands, use your teeth, use your mouth, use your voice.

Use your hands,
use your teeth,
use your mouth,
use your voice.

PLAYING SCALES

Most people set themselves tasks that are too big to achieve – a novel, an ambitious opera, an exhibition, a TV show.

Make it easier by reducing the scale of your ambition. Shrink the project to a series of micro-tasks.

Make the smallest of moves, like playing scales on the piano, miniscule tasks, to direct the eye or ear towards some minor, less ambitious goal.

An excellent way of achieving this is to do timed writing.

Try the following exercise.

The Exercise

Take ten minutes out of your day and write for that length of time (use a stopwatch to keep to the limits).

Don't worry about what you are writing. Simply keep the pen moving on the page.

Do this exercise every 24 hours, with no idea of output. Do it because you want to, because you need to physically experience writing.

Simply deliver your micro-tasks every day.

Refrain from looking back at what you have written. Simply add the texts together in a loose-leaf folder until thirty days have passed. Then review what you have made.

Speed is also useful. Our conscious mind has a tendency to direct us to more conservative choices. However, if we disrupt ourselves by working very fast, we have no opportunity to fall into familiar patterns.

In one of my last pieces, 'beginagain', I made 2,066 consecutive daily posts. I wrote until I couldn't write any more, until I was crushed by writing.

In the end, after those thousands of posts, my ability to write at top speed, about anything that happened in my day, was at its peak. I could sit down and simply download from my head all the thoughts from the last 24 hours in a coherent manner.

Even if we start with indecision and a lack of clarity, using this method, within thirty days, our writing can transform itself into something formidable, exact.

Ten minutes each day is all that you need to write your masterpiece.

Make the smallest of moves, like playing scales on the piano.

BLURRED PICTURES

I recently worked with an artist whose images were all
blurred – distorted colours, the camera pointing in the
wrong direction, objects badly aligned.

She was using this practice to experience real life
directly, empty of obstacles, moving straight towards
the feeling.

And doing this very successfully by being out of focus.

I found it very exciting.

It reminded me of the kinds of photographs that come
back from the lab with 'Error' stickers on them. When
I was making photos in an instamatic format, I would
rejoice if my images were returned with these failures
marked on them – it meant that my pictures weren't
ever framed in conventional ways.

Our drive towards clarity demands –

- The largest file size.
- The best camera.
- The clearest image.

However, this is usually a result of our mind taking
over, wanting to impose order on things, in a logical
way, before we have a chance to explore the material
more fully, in inexpert ways.

We want to add limits to our play before we have even begun.

Often, we are so afraid about the potential of our creativity that we need our outputs to be perfect, with no flaws. We want nothing to go wrong. So we buy the newest camera, the biggest screen, the fastest computer.

It's actually a relief to make work that cuts against the grain –

- Blurred photos.
- The backs of things.
- Upside down.
- Handwritten.
- Untrained voices.

Top Tip
Play with the taboo of imperfection; leave something incomplete.

Try to cultivate errors, mistakes.

You might find something in those blurred pictures, something you hadn't seen before.

In 'bad art' you might find your future salvation.

Play with the taboo of imperfection; leave something incomplete.

OFFENDING THE AUDIENCE

The less content you have in your work, the more exposing it will be.

After all, it's always you on the wall, or in the pages. Nothing is present in the material that isn't yourself.

Also, if the content is not figurative or descriptive, it will challenge the audience more and present a naked picture of you, whether you want to or not.

Sometimes, because we don't want to be exposed to this unflinching public gaze, we unconsciously police our own work, failing to adequately reveal things about ourselves in case of over-exposure.

It took me years to get this balance right – mixing biography and abstraction, conceptualism and disclosure.

Likewise, be careful of the pull towards conformity.

The drive towards consensus is often unacknowledged in us and makes us naturally incline towards the conservative.

- We want to please people.
- We want to repeat our successes.
- We want to be liked.

(I can find many items on this list that I've done before.)

The audience often wants you to simply repeat things that they recognise from your previous work.

We think that we can resist this...

However, the superego is so strong that, even if we believe that we are free, we are still heavily editing our own work, offering something that's acceptable to the viewer.

When I think about this fact, I always remember Peter Handke's play 'Offending The Audience'.

We should fly in the face of audience expectation and follow our own instinct.

We should laugh.

Even if it hurts.

We should fly
in the face
of audience
expectation
and follow our
own instinct.

UNIQUE EYE

UNIQUE EYE

I've always liked Charles Demuth's painting 'I Saw The Number 5 In Gold'.

It's the only artwork I know that uses the 'I' word, illustrating a way of seeing that is particular to CD.

I'm always grateful to Demuth for reproducing the image in this direct, uncomplicated and heroic way.

Inviting me to see what he sees.

It reminds me that our eye is unique. It directs each and every one of us to things that interest us.

Is it –

• A motorway flyover
• A ball
• A paper plane
• A dustbin
• A flower
• A long distance road
• A water hose
• A house?

What do you see?

Take these simple, unique observations and put them on paper. Use your pen as a cardiograph, the needle zigzagging a line on the printout, recording your heartbeat.

Whatever it is, write it down (it doesn't matter what you write).

- No one else sees like you.
- No one else experiences the world as you do.
- No one else feels like you.

If you have difficulty with this exercise, if you are struggling to think what is unique about you, write a list of your own abilities.

If your selection looks too meagre, ask some friends and colleagues to fill in the gaps, telling you about your positive qualities.

Often you think that everyone can do what you do.

Usually it's the opposite: no one has your exact expertise, a bundle of ideas and ways of behaving that are tied to your unique seeing of the world.

Sometimes we need other people to remind us of the qualities that we take for granted in ourselves.

- Can you take risks?
- Are you an ideas person?
- Do you have curatorial skills?
- Are you a good producer?

Ask your friends to fill in the blanks.

No one has your exact expertise.

ONE BOOK

There is only –

- One book
- One photo
- One song
- One play

that you can make.

It's in your style, with your voice, your tone.

Don't try to make it something else – it won't sell because it's not what you truly believe in.

Instead, keep it very simple.

- What you hear.
- What you believe.
- What you see.

There's actually nothing to creativity but this.

The thing that we always forget is that what makes us unique always works best. The generic, if we strive for it, in order to be popular, never succeeds.

For example, if we try to write a best-seller, it often doesn't work because we have no real interest in the mainstream.

(I have seen this many times.)

Therefore –

* Keep your uncommercial ideas.
* Keep the versions you throw out.
* Keep the controversial content.
* Keep the unsaleable projects.

It's often these unpolished elements that show the most originality.

Attempt to keep your output in liquid form, before it starts to resemble other things in the marketplace.

Always exhibit your last version but one. This script, slightly incomplete, with one or two flaws, will often be better than your polished, final output.

And leave at least one major error in the work.

Often it will improve the piece.

What makes us unique always works best.

NOTHING TO SAY (I DON'T BELIEVE YOU)

Sometimes I meet clients who believe that they have nothing to say.

Yet if challenged, if allowed to record what they see, they always discover interesting things about themselves.

For example, in one of my workshops, a participant chose a yellow counter, from a selection offered. She called it 'Lemon Sun', a quirky amalgam of two ideas stuck together.

This off-the-cuff remark offered her a useful title that she could take further, if she wanted to.

For example, if she recorded images of the sun every day, for a year, in all its detailed variety, her narrative would be original and spectacular.

But observation doesn't have to be about complication or volume.

The slightest things work –

- A personal narrative.
- Direct from you.
- With no interface.
- In simple language.

The Exercise

Try looking at something for one minute and notice
what you see.

Make a list of twenty observations and write them
down in your notepad, in order to concretise them on
the page before you forget.

See how long you can sustain this practice of looking.

Can it last five minutes, an hour, a day?

Observation doesn't have to be about volume. The slightest things work.

X-RAYS

The 'unique eye' technique I'm describing in this section is like the X-ray glasses that I used to see advertised in the back of comics.

These spectacles allegedly allowed you to look through people's clothes and see them naked.

However, the power of individual observation that I'm encouraging in you with this method results in the opposite effect. Instead of seeing other people, we get to see ourselves naked, with all our idiosyncrasies intact.

And all of these qualities are useful for being creative.

'Unique eye' represents our individual power and allows us to look through our own bones, like a radioactive slide, into the very core of our creativity, our cells, our DNA.

Whatever we see, however unusual, is what is us.

The world outside, with its revolving uncertainty, its whirlwind, is actually our inner life manifested as physical self.

I understood this, in a profound sense, when I went to stay at a Zen temple in Tokyo. The Master, Nishijima, told me that the supermarket around the corner, the one that I couldn't quite see from the window of his study, might not really exist.

It might be there, but it had no independent reality separate from me.

Everything I saw was my existence, my world – even this supermarket might be part of my own imagination.

Therefore, when I ask people to tell me what they see, I am interrogating them in a very deep way, asking them to look inside themselves.

Anything they focus on – a car, a newspaper, a piece of dirt, a house – is important to me, telling something about their current state of mind.

What's yours?

Whatever we see, however unusual, is what is us.

POOR ART

Overwhelmed by choices, it's hard to proceed. But with a selection of two, it's much easier.

Often I flip a coin in order to decide.

Heads or tails?

Recently I used this technique to complete a new work. In order to generate the pattern, rather than make one important decision, I made 420 smaller choices, each added together to complete the picture.

Out of a selection of 'poor' elements, I made something satisfyingly complex.

This process took me six hours (there is something about the difficulty that also contributed to the final output).

There are many creative systems that similarly limit personal choices – Dogme 95, haiku poetry, OuLiPo, Arte Povera, etc. These methods are all useful for taking you into spaces that are challenging and obverse.

If you don't normally experience this kind of poor culture, think about cultivating penury in an approximation of a forbidden style, one that's formed by what you don't have.

- Make it quickly.
- Use the leftovers.
- Halve the time spent.
- Scrape back.

All the best ideas are 'poor' i.e. they emerge out of necessity.

Top Tip

My own system for limiting behaviours is a series of rules that I sometimes apply to a new piece of work.

Ten Rules For Limiting Behaviours

- It begins obscure.
- Use dream information.
- Find your collaborators from a group of trained and untrained people.
- Cut the final output by 50%.
- Use chance.
- Include 'nonsense'.
- Part of it could be a game.
- The end might be contained in the beginning.
- Incorporate a personal challenge, however small.
- Cultivate empty space.

The last is perhaps the most important. Like Yves Klein's 'The Void', we step into the space of our imagination, each time looking for certainty.

(Klein's piece was actually an empty room.)

But there is, in fact, no such thing as 'us'.

Creativity is both imprecise and impermanent, lacking such definitions.

Yet we give it meaning by being there.

All the best
ideas are 'poor'
i.e. they emerge
out of necessity.

WRITE IT DOWN

There is a school of thought that believes that good ideas will stay in your head forever.

I don't believe this. Ideas are slippery and fluid. They need to be pinned to the page, like mounted butterflies in a case. With a flutter they will escape, to land in someone else's head, giving the idea to another person.

Even developed thoughts don't endure – I have lost thousands of them in my life.

So capture them before they are gone.

Many times I've been caught in compromising positions, writing down ideas on the paper place mats in Chinese restaurants or on an underground train scribbling notes directly on my hand in biro.

Or, worst of all, simply standing in the street, looking at something and writing my observations in a notepad, hardly mindful of pen on paper, so intent am I on getting the idea down before it evaporates.

In these situations, my acute embarrassment signals to those around me that I am prepared to be visible, to take a risk. I have stepped over a line and become vulnerable.

(The disregard of passersby is necessary for art to emerge.)

The Exercise

Try and make something out of all the ideas that have escaped you.

The forgotten titles, the scribbled bedside notes, the unintelligible script remaining after a night out.

Call it 'Gotaway'.

The disregard
of passersby is
necessary for
art to emerge.

I'M DRAWN TO IDEAS X, Y, Z

Often, we ameliorate the problems of being creative by placing barriers around ourselves that protect us against further difficulty.

Using the third person is one such device. It helps us deflect potential criticism by placing ourselves in a safer context.

We use the terms 'She/They/He/It' to give us a necessary distance.

(Sometimes we need the protection.)

If you are feeling somewhat stronger, instead try the first person. It's much more powerful. The 'I' cuts through and makes a bold, direct statement.

Like –

- I make…
- I'm interested in…
- I'm curious about…
- I feel…
- I see things this way…
- I'm drawn to ideas X, Y, Z…
- I'm enthusiastic about…
- I hope…
- I create…
- I work with…

Get the idea?

Usually it's our own enthusiasm about a project that inspires other people to be attracted to our ideas. In these circumstances, use the 'I' word to show your determination, commitment and drive.

Top Tip
At one point in my career, I refused to go to my own art openings, believing that they were simply opportunities for further harmful exposure.

Now, I believe that if I can't defend the work, who will? So I always attend. At the openings, if anyone ignores the material, I say 'Thank you' and move on to the next person, taking anything they say, however insignificant, as a compliment, regardless of the intention.

Thus the nonplussed 'Oh, YOU made it' is transformed by me into 'Isn't IT great.'

I do this with some humour; acting myself, playing a part.

I'm drawn to ideas X, Y, Z.

Y, Z, X.
Z, Y, X.
X, Z, Y.
Y, X, Z.
Z, X, Y.

It's all me and I am unafraid.

Use the 'I' word

to show your determination, commitment and drive.

SEEING

SEEING

I used to think that autobiography was the basic building block of all art, but now I realise that there's a prior state that comes even before our own story.

And that is seeing.

The eyes are a natural vortex, drawing impressions into us. However, we rarely acknowledge them, so conditioned are we to avoid looking.

Bombarded in the metropolis by visual information every day, we shut down to the image, so that few of our own impressions actually go in.

In the modern city, when do we have time to look at anything? We become denuded of experience and then suspicious of anything that comes along – through eye, hands or ear.

Once, when I was out walking in London, I was forced to shelter from a storm under the lit canopy of a cinema. Without a coat, I shuddered with cold. However, within minutes of the start of the thunder, I noticed that something strange was happening – the seconds became elastic, never-ending.

Time slowed down.

What formerly appeared as fragments, changed into huge vistas, disconnected from the physical.

The bright bulbs of the foyer were incandescent with electricity.

I suddenly understood that seeing was an active engagement, using the physical to leave the physical behind. I was heightened, transformed, moving into the storm-filled sky.

I realised that seeing requires a clear intention from us, a demand, an investment in the experience; not just a glance, but a pause, a moment, a reflection.

The bigger the personal commitment, the greater the meaning.

The Exercise

If we deliberately attempt to look at things, we can accumulate a lot of material from even the most meagre investment.

Find an object and build a visual relationship with it.

Try –

- A plate.
- A leaf.
- A penny.
- A face.
- A tree.
- A light.
- A car.

If all you can see is a wall, then look at the wall.

What happens?

If necessary, go back to the same object over and over again, getting a deeper idea of the visual impact of a particular thing.

Stare at something to step out of everyday reality into the deeper realm of self-absorption.

(Be careful of traffic.)

Seeing is
an active
engagement,
using the
physical to
leave the
physical
behind.

TABOO AGAINST LOOKING

It's very rare to be in a situation where we can just look.

Often, I feel it's not allowed; as if the act of looking is regarded as indulgent or counterproductive.

Looking generates nothing. It has no external output. Looking doesn't help define a product. It values no consumers. Therefore, in the modern world, we accord it little value.

Many times on my travels, out of simple curiosity, I've stopped to photograph a window, a garage, a doorway, a telephone box, and been regarded by passersby as quite eccentric.

'Why would you want to look at that?'

However, looking produces internal changes in us that are vital to our well-being, reviving us with fresh visual images.

There is a taboo in our culture against looking. It's possible for us to go to an art gallery, a football match or a firework display and watch something but outside these contexts we are not encouraged to look at things.

Yet the energy that rises up when we stare at something creates a radical feeling, a contact through our eyes that is unique.

Top Tip
In the street, look out for objects dropped on to the floor. Pay attention to anything that attracts your eye.

Immediately pick it up.

On the pavement I have discovered drawings, playing cards, dice – all of which have been integrated into my creative life in surprising and inventive ways.

Today I found three pieces of a child's jigsaw, left in the dirt.

Each describes a fragment of a cartoon world, brightly coloured. This treasure makes me excited, knowing that these scraps lead me forward into new spaces, in which I can imaginatively connect the disparate parts.

The pieces offer me a glimpse, a window into another life.

I put all three in my pocket.

The energy
that rises up
when we stare
at something
creates a
contact that
is unique.

WHAT DO I SEE?

What do I see, day after day, looking out of the window?

Today I see a hazy mountain, a dual carriageway leading off into the distance, a flowery chair.

Most of these things I don't really see because I have become habituated to the everyday reality around me.

The objects therefore become almost invisible. Yes, I see them, but they are really not there.

The world that I live in has to be navigated via shortcuts, so I am, in effect, looking through my eyes as if I am staring through a straw, so narrow is my focus. This is why I rarely hear myself say the phrase 'I see', because most of the time I am not really looking.

Yet if I want to enlarge this small sliver of attention, what can I do to bring a greater depth to my vision?

Firstly, I can consider seeing.

It's useful to turn the object upside down and shake it of its cultural certainty. I can look at a tree as a perch for birds.

I can detune my eyes and witness the whole world as one item, sheared of duality, regarding the landscape as a single entity, floating in concomitance.

Thus seeing becomes a meditation on the objects around me – a flowery chair, the trees, blossom, the relentless dual-lane carriageway.

Offering a way into the multi-sensory world that I have left behind.

It's useful to
turn the object
upside down
and shake it
of its cultural
certainty.

USE WHATEVER IS ALREADY THERE

It's often better to sift through the left-overs of previous work than fly off in search of other material.

We are always making and re-making.

(Don't leave anything to waste.)

Looking through some files, I found several of my previously abandoned projects –

- 'P.S.'
- 'Black Magic'
- 'Tricks'
- '13 Seasons'

They provided me with some very serviceable material, things I had forgotten about.

With every new project, I'm always fooled into believing that I can deliver the latest idea in under a year. Whilst this is perhaps a useful deceit to get the project going, it's a woefully inadequate time-frame.

Real complexity emerges out of struggle – the day-by-day accumulation of hope, failure and ecstasy.

We are always looking for a key to open the door.

(Usually we have forgotten that it's already in our hand.)

Real complexity emerges out of struggle.

IMAGES

AN OPENING INTO YOU

An image is an opening into you.

It invites me to step into your window.

Some of the best images I have seen are of the human face, providing a direct connection with the viewer, tapping into deep symbolic reserves within each one of us.

Use a photo of your own face.

Make it simple. Connect with the viewer in direct ways – eyes looking outwards from the frame.

Saying 'I am here.'

Thus the artist inside us can be witnessed by others in a simple way.

Put your face on the cover and the back of your head on the reverse, offering the audience a 360 degree profile of yourself, a 3-D view of what's inside.

(I did this on the sleeve of my first book, 'Tiny Stars'.)

The image is a direct way into you, the wound, the pierced side of your personality that gives you your power. The pictures that you create should celebrate this vital, profound wound.

Top Tip

If you can't find anything to photograph, turn the
camera on yourself.

Make you the subject.

This way you can intimately get to know your own self.

Videotape your eyes, your hand, your feet walking,
your shout.

If you can't find anything to photograph, turn the camera on yourself.

DRAW APPROXIMATIONS

Thinking about an image should be simultaneous with the generation of a project and ought to develop alongside its key stages, rather than be a last minute addition.

This cultivates a pictorial sense in you, so when you need to create a promotional photograph for a particular exhibition, you are already further advanced in your thinking about images.

Pictures grow out of process. They aren't simply added at the end of the journey, like icing on a cake.

So when you come to the output, it will be a question of making a selection, rather than starting from scratch.

Try to –

- Keep a visual diary.
- Collect colour.
- Borrow from the masters.
- Amass props.
- Make sketchbooks.
- Use fashion.
- Draw approximations.

It's not the cost of images that counts, rather the imaginative overturning that you signal by your choice of idea.

Turn it upside down, add an inventive subtitle, expose something.

(Embarrassment is necessary.)

Top Tip
If you can't do any of these things, then license a library image. Here at least you will be able to buy into high production values for a fraction of the price.

When using these for-hire photos, place them in unusual relationships to your subject matter, dislocating the connection between idea and representation.

For example, one of my favourite Pelican book covers is for 'Yoga' by Ernest Wood (1970). Here, the designer has turned a photo of a face upside down on the cover, thereby mimicking the contents inside.

Simple but very effective.

Embarrassment
is necessary.

THE DESERT

Recently I was looking at Marc Camille Chaimowicz's piece 'Le Désert' (1981), created out of the fragments of a previous photograph, cut up with scissors.

It reminded me how sophisticated very simple elements can be.

The subtlety comes from slight accumulations, elegant manipulations of tiny details, over and over again, delivered in a masterful way.

Your role as an artist is to marshal these ordinary elements: taking away, mixing, subtracting.

Many times artists come to me and ask me how to start making work. I say use whatever is to hand, however inauspicious these materials might appear – cardboard, smashed glass, dust.

Perhaps you are laughing; thinking how could a practice be created from crushed glass? That is your job, to discover how to make these pyramids of glass come alive.

MCC's piece 'Le Désert' is an accurate title. It suggests that we are always working with scraps, remainders of the event, a desert, in order to assemble a new image from what is in front of us.

There is no big picture.

That is why in this section I run out of big ideas, like my printer runs out of ink.

Yellow...
Blue...
Orange...
Pink...

The colour stops here.

The Exercise

Photocopy an existing work, then chop it up into pieces, not paying any attention to the places where you cut.

Reassemble the parts using different criteria –

- Size.
- Abstract qualities.
- Shadows.
- White space.
- Detail.

Use this new version as the basis for your next piece.

Rather than starting from the figurative each time, make experiments with abstraction, making these further adaptions your new in-point.

Your role as an artist is to marshal these ordinary elements: taking away, mixing, subtracting.

WILD HORSES ON THE WALL

It's often useful to work with what's left, even if this means beginning at a point of confusion, within the unknown.

For example, if, as has happened to me before, I find two people staying behind at the end of a workshop, I often encourage them to exchange contact details with each other because there might be a reason that they are both there at the same time.

Thus a person becomes the found object.

Similarly, in one exercise I ask my workshop participants to bring along an image that they have found the previous week. After the session, many of these pictures are abandoned on the floor. So I often collect up what's left there and take it home.

At the moment I have a photo above my desk, found in this way, of a wild horse being ridden by a stetson-wearing cowboy at a rodeo.

I like to turn this magazine image upside down and on its side, where it looks like a map of the United States, transformed from its original meaning, like a Rorschach inkblot test, into a Rothko or a Motherwell painting.

I don't understand why I saved this particular photograph of a cowboy – the meaning has yet to emerge.

But that's OK. I can enjoy this image, until a time comes when I can put him in a more logical context.

Perhaps this will never happen...

It reminds me that being lost, especially within the image, is actually alright for me.

We often seek out certainty but it's within our dream-like relationship with images where most of the work gets done.

Top Tip
Never try and tidy up for the viewer.

Leave the work ragged, unpredictable. Here, in its formless experimentalism, complexity accumulates.

Start your script at the point of confusion.

Let it be like life; always looking for the bigger picture, but never quite catching it.

It's within our dream-like relationship with images where most of the work gets done.

FOUND MATERIAL

The relationship to discarded material is charged, electric.

It's my unconscious forcefully directing me to what I'm interested in – through the things that I see all around me.

Often, in the city, I become glued to the pavement, with a strong sense that something new is going to arrive: a red Lego brick, a ring-pull, a plastic bottle top.

Amassed day after day, these objects alert me to what's happening in my creative life.

They are talismanic presences.

However, sometimes I filter things out, I police my own work by pretending that I am not really excited by the things that I see. This is because we are taught not to trust ourselves, to disbelieve in our first impressions.

So I struggle to save the ring-pull from the can of soft drink in the gutter, or I wait until someone passes by before I pick it up, somewhat shamefaced.

But it's useful to note how difficult it often is to follow your instincts when everyone is telling you that you are misguided.

Top Tip
Don't be ashamed of your own choices.

They can't endlessly be avoided.

What gets ignored comes back in later life to find you, more determined than ever.

The ring-pull opens you up, like a can of pop, quietly revealing what's inside, whether you want to discover it or not.

Don't be ashamed of your own choices.

LE 'C' DREAM

Last night I dreamt of a Le Corbusier project in France that doesn't actually exist.

Although this building complex had been widely praised in the architectural community, it was also noted that it benefited from a spectacular natural setting – off the shore was a luxuriant island with three dramatic jagged peaks rising up out of the jungle.

I have no idea what this dream means (although I can take a good guess).

In one sense it doesn't matter.

It becomes another visual resource for me: an island inside of my psyche, always fertile and exotic, building internal landscapes, within the natural setting that's myself.

The dream could have been –

- A performing whale.
- Wittgenstein.
- A cannon at a fairground.
- Patterns.
- Jim Carrey's house.
- Electricity cables.

If so, I would work with those pictures instead.

More and more I find myself attempting to access my unconscious as a place where new, important images can be found.

Here, as on the street, I can locate the discarded and bright parts of my personality and integrate them into my new work.

The directness of these pictures, unmediated by my ego, is often refreshing and alive.

Top Tip
If you are writing several narratives simultaneously, it's likely that they are all parts of the same piece, however bizarre that might seem.

It will all be one novel, one book.

Anything that comes in, within a given period, I accept, as if it were meant to happen.

- Confusion?
- Injudicious language?
- Lack of connection?
- Ridiculous scale?
- Loss of story?

I use it all.

Stimulate this dream-like parallelism by attempting to read several books at the same time – texts, visual monographs, recipes, art histories.

Anything that comes in, within a given period, I accept, as if it were meant to happen.

THE REVERSE

I collect images from a variety of sources: magazines, colour charts, postcards – anything that catches my eye.

I save these in transparent folders.

The see-through pages allow a collision of images to occur, leaving the reverse visible. Sometimes, the combination of these elements can be surprising; the transparent sleeves encourage multiple connections to emerge, ones that I had never originally envisaged.

Likewise, in one workshop I ran, a man brought several photographs, all taken from a Dutch magazine. However, my eye was drawn to the headline on the reverse of the image:

'Ik zou met u in contact willen blijven.' (I would like to stay connected to you.)

It reminded me that often what's adjacent can also be helpful to us.

Our unconscious mind allows us access to a range of material, some of which we might not understand. This 360 degree spectrum can be composed of complex, paradoxical, even confusing elements, all of which are useful to the creative person.

Even the reverse of an image can be something worthy of our attention.

'I would like to stay connected to you' tells the participant useful information about his current state, if he chooses to follow this trajectory.

However, this material is around us all the time. Most of it we block out because we can't deal with the deluge of detail coming towards us. Yet, if we can look at the reverse, there are useful clues found here, ideas that might change our fixed concept of our self, if we want to attempt it.

Top Tip
Collect folders dedicated solely to images and separate files for writing. Keep apart. Then after thirty days, mix the two, placing an image with a title, some text with a photograph.

What connections are made?

This way you can discover what you are really interested in – colours, names, concepts, titles.

Be uncritical of these first experiments.

Piece them together in instinctive ways, unafraid of the shapes that you make. Keep moving them around until you discover something that you like.

Even the reverse of an image can be something worthy of your attention.

I SEE

A GLASS ON A TABLE

I look at a glass of water in front of me.

What I see can't be shared or divulged with anyone else. I can try to describe it, however, I can't look at it in the same way as another person, because it's based on my own unique vision.

My singular glass.

Zen monk Kōshō Uchiyama describes this situation perfectly in his translation of Dōgen's 'Bendowa'. He says that we can't transfer our reality – it is ours alone.

When we are born, we bring it into being and when we die, we take it with us.

Therefore the glass on the table is different for each of us. We each have an idiosyncratic view of this object – the colour, the contents, the shape.

Rather than a problem, I see this as an advantage. Our eyes are tuned to different things, creating in each of us an alternate reality. We are each living in our own unique world.

This difference is the beginning of art.

The empty tumbler sitting on the green tablecloth. How do I look at this? What are the zigzag ideas behind my eyes?

I see –

- Glass as alternate.
- Empty as different.
- Table as individual.

Like a Malevich, an Imi Knoebel or a Barnett Newman.

We often say that artists reorganise reality in their work, make a world. Rather, I believe that it's more accurate to say that artists record what they actually, physically see through their eyes, with all the visual imperfections left intact.

But first, as creative people, in order to achieve this, to offer it to others, we have to believe in our own original vision, so that we can share what we see.

We need to –

- Look.
- Authenticate.
- Experience.
- Value.

(This can take a lifetime.)

The eyes are old wounds (I talk about myself here), directing the experience of the world through physical and metaphysical reality.

What do I see?

- Radio.
- Minutes.
- Sun.
- Balloon.
- Corporeal.
- Yellow.
- Superimpose.
- America.

(All taken at random from my current notepad and so a snapshot of what's happening to me now.)

The glass on the table is different for each of us.

RODS

I once read that the rods in your eyes change and
deteriorate over time. So the colour seen at age 12
is not the same as that seen at 68.

Our eyes change, our bodies mutate and what we
thought was real turns out to be only partial, incomplete.

I can believe this.

My perception of blue is less clear than it once was,
due to my short-sightedness. However, perhaps it's
also more profound than what I once saw as a child.
It has become more symbolic.

The tempering of time gives my sky this quality of
experience, full of meaning; a reading that comes with
age – impossible to transfer to another human being.

The sky festooned with clouds, like a Flemish
painting, floats in the reality of my not-really-seeing-it.

My blue sky is solemn, light, impersonal, serene.

I pick up a piece of old curtain with a pattern of blue
flowers and leaves that I bought in a charity shop. The
hem is unstitched, sheared by sharp scissors.

This colour has the same sky blue of Willem van de
Velde, a colour so chaste it is reminiscent of all skies
in the world.

I hold the cloth in front of my eyes, so the whole room turns blue.

The colour seen at age 12 is not the same as that seen at 68.

I SEE A PALM TREE

In 2001 I made 'Windows' for the BBC – an online essay.

As part of the project, I asked the readers to leave their computer, go to the nearest window and email me a message with a description of what they saw.

These replies were sent direct to the BBC and then months later passed on to me, so by the time they arrived I had almost forgotten about the exercise.

The first reply that I read simply said, 'I see a palm tree'.

At the time I found this indefatigably exotic – a vision of reality quite different from my own; certainly not the grey and rainy London of that time.

It also reminded me of the power of 'I see'.

Within this place of 'seeing', narrative can be empty, an ongoing chain of relationships, each unique, separate from another, but linked together through the power of 'I'.

In fact, a series of 'I sees', recorded as daily impressions, can make up the contents of a book.

All you need to do is hold up a mirror to what's in front of you.

Not the 'I see' of someone else, but our own real 'I see'.

In this case a palm tree.

There are many ways of achieving this – here is one method.

The Exercise

Go out on to the street for five minutes and note down what you see. In your mind's eye, upend the objects or turn them 90 degrees. What kinds of shapes do they make?

Or turn yourself to see the sky or the pavement from a different angle.

Then come back.

Tell me, what did you find?

Over time, after many weeks, these simple 'I see' exercises of discovery and evaluation, of experiment and chance, can help to build a practice that is genuine, unique.

And after a while we can use this idiosyncratic way of seeing things to direct other people towards our singular reading of the world.

You are now on your way to being an 'artist', using the world as a prism.

Top Tip
Be a camera.

Record what you see automatically, in long takes, as if you are making a 24 hour film of your life, in parallel to your actual existence.

Edit later (or not at all).

- I see a house.
- I see a light.
- I see clouds.
- I see a window.
- I see a glass.
- I see rooftops.

The exotic solar flare of 'I see a palm tree' is still resounding in my head after several years.

Record what
you see
automatically,
in long takes,
as if you are
making a 24
hour film of
your life.

LONG STORIES

My eyes were opened by the power of 70s cinema to actual stories that recorded in real time the passage of life.

So –

- Unbroken camera shots.
- Actual locations.
- Real time recording.
- Little dialogue.

These long, rambling stories inspired me.

In these works of the avant-garde, the filmmakers had no concept of cross-cutting, or simultaneous action. Instead, the narrative is flat and monotone, with little or no subtext; a meeting, not of logic, but inspired, Neanderthal deliberateness.

So, for example, when I see, in Wim Wenders' film 'Summer In The City', the camera trained in real time on a man having some passport photographs of himself taken in a photo booth, the flash of the machine bulb illuminating the scene, I know that this is how 'I see' works, making an image from what's actually there – in this case Munich 1970.

What is your flash-bulb illumination?

Remember that your work could last –

- One hour.
- Three days.
- A week.
- Several years.

There is no limit.

There is no correct way to be creative. Everything that is really interesting is quite the opposite, full of errors and holes. An erratic mixture, the sole province of one unique vision – a singular maker.

In order to get in touch with this again, make long stories, narratives that expose you to feelings that would be hidden away in more conservative work.

Abandon structure until it resembles something like your real life.

(I'm thinking of the scene in Andrei Tarkovsky's 'Stalker' where the protagonist lies face down for several minutes in the long grass, breathing in its sweetness.

This shot needs no other explanation, no dialogue and no camera movement to distract the viewer from the intense feelings that it provokes.)

Top Tip

Make work between the 'I' and the 'see', where the ideas become thin, like a balloon blown up too big, alerting you to areas of obvious visibility, where you can pop the skin and so release the energy inside yourself.

There is no correct way to be creative.

LASER CONE

When I visited a retrospective of Nam June Paik in Düsseldorf, I spent some time lying down under his sculpture 'Laser Cone'.

As the neon lights flickered impulsively across the fabric of the tent, flat on my back, I surrendered to the pulse of the laser and experienced a temporary floating, a giving-up of my will, that was very seductive.

It reminded me that surrender is a useful technique for developing creativity.

This collapse is often signposted in me by a period of depression or illness. This crash finally forces me to give up. Many times, at this exact moment, a solution arrives, quite disconnected from the source of the original problem.

I now see my own surrender as an opportunity to engage with my unconscious in antithetical ways, not controlled by logic.

Only within the temporary crash of the ego is this possible.

I can also momentarily simulate this effect by doing exactly what I did at the Nam June Paik exhibition – lying on the floor.

(I try to do this now.)

Even without Paik's neon fireworks, my consciousness floats agreeably in the upside down world. I see the ceiling as my reality, yet I am still supported by the ground in real and substantial ways.

It's magnificent.

Try it (taking, of course, all the usual precautions).

The abandonment of logic in this way facilitates different methods of thinking about the world, turning reality on its head.

Try –

- An older technical format
- Handmade
- A photocopied output
- Signs on cardboard
- A dramatically reduced budget

in order to 'see' upside down.

It's the idea that counts, not the form.

If I had waited until I had the perfect mechanism for delivering creative products, I would never have begun anything. Instead, I would have tried to find the ideal context for my work, the best publisher and therefore never released any books.

And you wouldn't be reading this.

Surrender is a useful technique for developing creativity.

ISHIHARA

I'm red/green colour-blind.

I find that I have a problematic relationship to all colours, especially in poor light. The Ishihara Colour Test, used to check for colour-blindness, is therefore something with which I'm very familiar.

I can't see anything in these visual examinations: it's all a blank to me.

I once saw a building on the corner of the street being repainted – a dazzling display of red and purple, until I realised that this was only a cheap undercoat. The final colour, added days later, was a sober black, the colours hidden underneath layers of sombre gloss.

This made me laugh, realising my lack of visual acuity.

Try to substitute inappropriate colours, as if you're choosing them in the dark, so you don't know what you are using, thereby avoiding a conventional sense of visual balance.

Who cares about the correct way of seeing?

If you can only see the canvas upside down, with holes, back to front or in tiny pieces – that is your absolute right.

Don't deny it.

Try to substitute inappropriate colours, as if you're choosing them in the dark.

EVERYONE
IS CREATIVE

ART IS...

Art is easy...

However, being an artist is more difficult. It requires discipline, bravery, originality and perseverance.

(None of these are easily won.)

To accomplish these goals, focus on your day-to-day creativity, rather than attempting to make 'Art' with a capital 'A'. If you follow this modest path of everyday achievement, you won't go far wrong.

Forget all sorts of fixation with creating products; it won't help you. Instead, invest in a daily process as the mainstay of your practice.

Look at things – even if this first appears difficult. Keep your eyes open all your life; look at shapes, faces, colours, lights.

Even if there's 'nothing there', even if there's a brick wall, or grey clouds, there is always something worth looking at.

Trust your 'unique eye', your original seeing of the world. It's the basis of all art and the centre of your creativity.

Your world is unique, intrinsic to you.

Focus on your day-to-day creativity, rather than attempting to make 'Art' with a capital 'A'.

RHODODENDRONS

In order to find a way to conclude this book, I decided to try to write a list of twenty things that I believe in.

Here it is –

- I believe in me.
- I believe in portable realities.
- I believe in perception.
- I believe in the reliability of seeing.
- I believe in you.
- I believe in your answers.
- I believe in the power of good.
- I believe in the experimental.
- I believe in our ability not to judge ourselves.
- I believe in chance principles.
- I believe in found things.
- I believe in my own way of finding answers.
- I believe in the collective unconscious.
- I believe in good information.
- I believe in the reverse.
- I believe in simplicity.
- I believe in the inverse of anxiety (shake it off).
- I believe in the senses.
- I believe in one thing.
- I believe in now.

(And the opposite of all these things.)

So, forced to name the things that I do believe in, I am able to draw this book to a close.

Through the 50s curtain by the window, composed of pale lemon and grey cross stitching, I look out on to a different world, a space that a moment ago was 'existence' – now it's a place of 'I believe'.

A line of bricks, pink rhododendron flowers, blue sky, a sloping mountain terrain.

This must be my belief system, for this is my own reality.

The Exercise

Only let in visual information.

Ignore anything that pertains to text or writing. Put your language blinkers on, avoid the newspapers and strike out the impact of the word.

(Try it for 24 hours – it's a very hard practice to sustain.)

Don't give this visual input a value, just let it be images, colour or tone.

Stop ascribing meaning to your observations, simply allow sense impressions of the world to impact on you.

Surrender to the information received by your eyes.

Released from the word, forced to rebuild a relationship with your surroundings, what happens to your world?

Only let in visual information.

DIRTY WATER

Look for a second at something – let it absorb you.

Within this 'I see' world of phenomena, all things become still. Time expands. What you imagine was merely a second becomes all seconds, all time; the duration of your lifetime.

Try it and see.

I try to do this exercise myself, experience it by picking up a book at random off my desk, a mock-up, all white, and weigh it in my hands, looking at it.

It's empty (all the pages are blank). Even in this void state, it represents as much a truth as anything else I'm looking for.

For example, I could read Gilles Deleuze, P.D. Ouspensky or Merleau-Ponty (all writers on perception), but in the end there's no need to learn anything. All esoteric knowledge comes down to being just an articulation of another's experience; not my own world at all.

So perhaps the best solution is simply to give up.

In this state of egolessness, of discovery, the phenomena of the world become our allies – instead of something we are constantly fighting against.

It's simple – look and keep looking and something will arrive.

When you stay with the long-term challenges of 'I see', things always turn up.

Invest in the discipline of looking.

Study –

- Dirty water.
- Breakages.
- Concrete.
- Piles of sand.
- Shadows.
- Car fumes.

Why not?

Invest in the discipline of looking.

THE FOUNTAIN

You don't need money to be an artist.

We are convinced by the system that creativity needs finance, because that's the model that we are all working within. However, the more I think about it, the more I see creativity as something quite different, something that can't be bought and sold.

It's a fountain, a spring.

This fountain is not necessarily reliant on money. In fact, it can't be contained in that way. It moves around, changing location, much to the annoyance of people who try to bottle it.

The spring is free.

(This idea is from C.G. Jung, retold by Robert A. Johnson in his book 'Owning Your Own Shadow'.)

Money can be used to validate work from outside sources (funders, dealers, patrons etc.) but it's not essential in order to make something.

In fact, it's counterproductive to think of your creativity as a fixed product that can be bought and sold.

I've previously used all sorts of metaphors to describe creativity: radio waves, stitching, pinned butterflies, a series of steps.

Creativity is none of these things; it's formless, inchoate and obeys no particular master, save the self.

It's nothing other than what you see in the world, mapped extensively on the page.

Put as much energy into developing your ability to see as you would invest in filling in applications for funding. The latter will drain your creativity (in the same way as bottling the fountain). However, if you can 'see', it's possible to lead the way, to make a visionary relationship to art, using the values of the sublime.

This can have a profound impact on others, encouraging personal change within them and an altered view of their own surroundings.

It's definitely something worth doing.

I believe in the power of 'I see' and its ability to transform what's around us.

I believe in 'I believe'.

Creativity is formless, inchoate and obeys no particular master, save the self.

CLOSE YOUR EYES

Finally...

Close your eyes. What images can you see behind your eyelids?

Spend some seconds looking inside. Here in the place of absorption and isolation, you can find all the images that you need.

Is it a colour, a place, a feeling, a shape?

Trust that 'seeing' requires no equipment, no large investment, no complex collaboration and no technical mastery.

Everything can be accomplished simply by closing your eyes.

Here the journey of the artist at last comes to an end – gathered from original impressions hidden behind the eyes. Invest in this world every day to augment your practice, always waiting for the good idea, the next impulse to arrive.

The eye is an iris, a frisbee, a car wheel, a 45 rpm record.

See what it sees...

Everything can be accomplished simply by closing your eyes.

MICHAEL ATAVAR

Michael Atavar is an artist and a creative consultant with a practice that mixes creativity, business, art and psychology.

His output includes over thirty public works, in a variety of forms – performance, installation, digital media, publishing.

www.atavar.com
www.how-to-be-an-artist.com
www.12-rules-of-creativity.com
www.everyone-is-creative.com
www.creativepractice.com
www.210cards.com

ACKNOWLEDGEMENTS

This book was written using '210CARDS', a creative card system by Michael Atavar and Miles Hanson.

Thank you to Allan, Erik, Helen, Julian, Martin, Miles, Pat, Richard, Ritchie, Roelof, Ruth, Sandra, Steven. Thanks to all the staff at the Tate Modern Bookshop.

Special thanks to Jonathan Kemp and Gabriella Clara Larsen for editorial insight.

Section diagrams by Richard Scarborough, Latin motto by Nicholas Field.

Many thanks to all the workshop participants and group members referred to in this text.

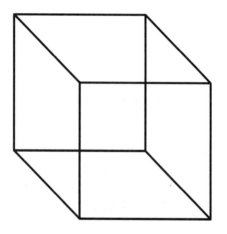